AMAZING AEROPLANES

D1340086

For Jan and Billy – T.M.
For Henry and Horace – A.P.

The Publisher thanks the British Airways Community Learning Centre at
Heathrow Airport in London for their kind assistance in the development of this book.

🐦 KINGFISHER

First published by Kingfisher 2002
This edition published by Kingfisher in 2007
an imprint of Macmillan Children's Books
a division of Macmillan Publishers Limited
20 New Wharf Road, London N1 9RR
Basingstoke and Oxford
Associated companies throughout the world
www.panmacmillan.com

ISBN: 978-0-7534-1488-0

Text copyright © Tony Mitton 2002 Illustrations copyright © Ant Parker 2002
The moral right of the author and illustrator has been asserted.

All rights reserved. No part of this publication may be reproduced, stored in or introduced
into a retrieval system, or transmitted, in any form or by any means (electronic, mechanical,
photocopying, recording or otherwise), without the prior written permission of the publisher.
Any person who does any unauthorized act in relation to this publication may be liable to criminal
prosecution and civil claims for damages.
3 5 7 9 10 8 6 4 2

A CIP catalogue record for this book is available from the British Library.

Printed in China

This book is sold subject to the condition that it shall not, by
way of trade or otherwise, be lent, resold, hired out, or
otherwise circulated without the publisher's prior consent
in any form of binding or cover other than that in
which it is published and without a similar
condition including this condition being
imposed on the subsequent purchaser.

AMAZING AEROPLANES

Tony Mitton and Ant Parker

KINGFISHER

Whoosh

An aeroplane's amazing,
for it travels through the sky,

above the clouds, for miles and miles,
so very fast and high!

An airport is the place you go
to take a trip by air.

You check in at the terminal to show you've paid your fare.

The ground crew weigh your baggage
and load it in the hold.

And then you take the walkway to the plane,
when you are told.

The flight deck's where the captain
and co-pilot do their jobs.
They both know how to fly the plane
with all its dials and knobs.

They radio Control Tower to check
the runway's clear.
They can't take off unless it is,
with other planes so near.

By intercom, the captain on the flight deck
says hello.

You have to do your seat belt up,
before the plane can go!

A plane is big and heavy,
yet it climbs up really high.

It zooms along the runway
and soars into the sky.

Its wings hold big jet engines,
which are loud and very strong.
They suck in air and blow it through
to whoosh the plane along.

When the plane moves fast enough,
the air around's so swift
it pushes up beneath the wings
and makes the whole plane lift.

Soon the plane is in the air,
so now you're on your flight.
The cabin crew look after you
and see that you're all right.

They bring you drinks and magazines
and trays of food to eat.
And sometimes there's a film to watch
while sitting in your seat.

When the journey's over,
the captain lands the plane.
Control Tower have to say it's safe
for coming down again.

You sit with seat belt fastened,
there's a bumpy, rumbling sound –
the wheels are making contact
and the plane is on the ground!

At last the doors are opening.
Then out you come with smiles.

So give a cheer! For look, you're here.
You've flown for miles and miles.

Aeroplane bits

control tower

from here the air traffic controllers direct the planes and tell pilots when to take off and land safely

flight deck

sometimes called the **cockpit** this is where the pilot and co-pilot sit

wheel

the wheels fold away while the plane is in the air

hold

this is the space where heavy luggage is stored

wing →

the wings are hollow to make them as light as possible and a smooth shape so they move through the air easily

jet engine

jet engines blow out air and gas to push the plane forward – the gas is made by burning fuel

terminal

this is the building at the airport where passengers go to catch a plane

TERMINAL